50.00

TEACH
C

cknowledgment

II1050877

THE ROLE OF CLASS DISCUSSION IN THE LEARNING-CENTERED CLASSROOM

K. Patricia Cross

The Cross Papers
Number 6

March 2002

League for Innovation in the Community College
Educational Testing Service

Acknowledgment

The Educational Testing Service (ETS) has been a key partner in League projects and activities for well over a decade. We are indebted to ETS for its generous contributions to the preparation and publication of the sixth paper in the League's annual series, "The Cross Papers." With support from ETS this paper will be distributed to thousands of community college leaders around the world.

ISBN 1-931300-32-1

FOREWORD

Pat Cross has focused on learning throughout her career, so when ideas of learning-centered education came to the forefront of the community college reform discussion almost a decade ago, she was far ahead of many of us. Knowing her commitment to community colleges and recognizing the rich value of her experience, the League asked Pat to join our Learning Initiative and share her wisdom with community college faculty through a series of annual Cross Papers. She graciously accepted and has been a regular contributor to our conversations on learning each year through this engaging and eminently practical monograph series.

Despite the attention learning-centered education has received in recent years, the idea of education focusing on learning is hardly radical, nor is it the exclusive domain of educational theorists and reformers. In this paper, Pat takes the ideas of learning-centered education straight to the classroom, where she turns them into practical strategies for improving teaching and learning. Moreover, in this sixth addition to the series, Pat acknowledges a fundamental reality of higher education: the lecture format is the most frequently used method of instruction and it isn't likely to go away. Rather than joining the chorus of those who bemoan the lecture as a one-way knowledge delivery system, she encourages faculty to make their lectures more interactive. And, in her usual, pragmatic style, she provides a repertoire of simple techniques for engaging students in learning-centered classroom dialogue.

During the six years Pat has been writing these papers, she has covered such topics as classroom assessment, collaboration, and motivation, always with learning as the intended outcome. She writes directly to faculty, offering practical strategies for the rookie as well as the veteran. We hope this newest paper on the role of discussion in the classroom will stimulate conversations among you and your colleagues as you look for ways to improve and expand learning for your students, and perhaps for yourselves as well.

Mark David Milliron, President & CEO
Cynthia Wilson, Vice President, Publications & Research
League for Innovation in the Community College

THE ROLE OF CLASS DISCUSSION IN THE LEARNING-CENTERED CLASSROOM

K. Patricia Cross

What is a learning-centered classroom? Terry O'Banion (1999) observes that while the terms "learner-centered" and "learning-centered" are often used interchangeably, they do not mean the same thing. He highlights the difference by the use of an analogy in which a person goes to a spa for a week to lose five pounds. Although he is welcomed, regarded with great respect, showered with attention, and treated with the latest advances in equipment and facilities, at the end of the week when he steps on the scale, he is dismayed to find that he has not lost a single pound. O'Banion concludes, "He has paid a high price for a learner-centered experience, but did not achieve his learning-centered goal of losing five pounds."

Although community colleges have no desire to provide a pampered spa experience for their students, community colleges do take justifiable pride in making students feel welcome, important, and the *raison d'etre* for the college. While centering attention on learners and their needs and hopes may be important–even essential to the mission of the community college–it is not enough. Robert Barr and John Tagg (1995) made a profound impression, not only on community colleges, but on all higher education, when they proclaimed that colleges exist not solely to "provide instruction," but to "produce learning." By titling their article in *Change*, "From Teaching to Learning," they inadvertently led some to believe that teaching is diminished in favor of learning–which only goes to show how no good deed goes unpunished. But the concept of learning-centered classrooms makes it clear that learning is the task, and teachers and students are jointly responsible for creating and maintaining an environment in which learning is encouraged, valued, and accomplished. So, on to the second question: What do we know about learning and how to "produce" it?

We live in an era of exceptional excitement and promise for educators. We know more about learning than anyone in history has ever known, and scientists continue to explore the mysteries of the brain, with its infinite capacity for growth and change from–quite literally–the womb to the tomb. At present, there is more interest in the development of the brain at the extremes of the age continuum–from pre-birth to after-death autopsies of Alzheimer's patients–than in the middle years that are the major concern of educators. Perhaps the results are less splashy and spectacular than demonstrations of the neural connections of the brain, but cognitive science has been making progress of its own in understanding learning in 8- to 80-year-olds. The work that shows special promise for improving practice rises from studies of the correlates of learning. The question for this research is, "What are the conditions most likely to produce learning?" It is a practical and answerable question, one that is central to the design of learning-centered classrooms.

The let's-get-serious-about-learning movement started in 1983 when the most widely publicized report on education ever written warned that "the educational foundations of our society are presently being eroded by a rising tide of mediocrity that threatens our very future as a nation and a people" (National Commission on Excellence in Education, 1983, p. 5). Four years later, a group of educational scholars and researchers convened to cull from the voluminous research of the past 50 years those conclusions that would be most useful in addressing the need for improving learning in the nation's colleges. Their report, titled "Seven Principles of Good Practice in Undergraduate Education" (Chickering & Gamson, 1987), set forth seven conditions for learning. Good practice, it said,

1. encourages student-faculty contact
2. encourages cooperation among students
3. encourages active learning
4. gives prompt feedback
5. emphasizes time on task
6. communicates high expectations
7. respects diverse talents and ways of learning

Solid research shows that these are the conditions under which learning is most likely to take place. "While each practice can stand on its own," wrote the authors of the report, "when all are present, their effects multiply. Together, they employ six powerful forces in education." Those forces are:

- Activity
- Cooperation
- Diversity
- Expectations
- Interaction
- Responsibility

I am going to use these six forces, identified through research to be critically important in producing learning, as the organizing framework for some remarks on how to maximize learning through class discussion which, for better or for worse, is the most common pedagogical method in use today and through the ages.

Strategy in Classroom Discussion

Despite growing criticism of the traditional lecture/discussion format, it remains the overwhelming method of choice among college teachers. And there is really nothing wrong with it if it is used with the conscious and express purpose of promoting learning. The problem is that most teachers simply teach as they were taught, telling what they know and hoping that students will be interested enough to learn. The limitations of formal lecturing as an effective pedagogy have been so well publicized recently that most teachers are aware of the necessity to involve students actively in learning. Yet research shows that even when they think they are not lecturing, but rather conducting class discussion, teachers are doing 80 percent of the talking!

Class discussion covers a wide range of learning sins and virtues. Some teachers use discussion to promote learning; others use it to fill class time. Some discussion is carefully planned; some occurs by default. Some challenges and engages students; some bores. Some is task-oriented; some lacks any focus. Some is learner-centered; most is teacher-centered. And some discussion consists largely of questions and answers, with a call for "right answers," while some is more like a conversation, challenging analysis and higher-level thinking skills. In short, class discussions can offer powerful learning experiences, but they can also be deadly, stifling time wasters. They can trivialize learning and discourage rather than promote it.

What should a learning-centered discussion look like? I suggest that it should look something like a winning basketball team. The six forces for producing learning that have been identified in research are similar to the forces that are apparent in winning a team sport. Certainly, a winning coach is going to go into the game expecting to win; she is going to hold **high expectations** for performance. She will foster **active engagement** in the game and **cooperation** and **interaction** among team members, and she will cultivate **diversity**, nurturing and capitalizing on the distinctive talents of each member of the team. Moreover, a winning coach is going to demand that all players assume **responsibility** for keeping in shape, for showing up for practice, and for doing their personal best in each and every game. A successful coach knows the game and knows it well, but she uses lecture and demonstration sparingly, knowing that whatever talents she has or had as a player, she cannot transfer them to her players. The only way for players to develop and improve their skills is to get in there and practice the winning moves themselves.

Discussion is uniquely designed to encourage students to strengthen their intellectual muscle and practice their strategic learning moves. It can be a very powerful and useful teaching and learning strategy. Perhaps that is why it has lasted so long. Less clear is how it has endured with so few masters of the art.

C. Roland Christensen, professor emeritus of the Harvard Business School, is a recognized master of the art of teaching by the discussion method. He contends that discussion is especially effective "when educational objectives focus on qualities of mind (curiosity, judgment, wisdom), qualities of person (character, sensitivity, integrity, responsibility), and the ability to apply general concepts and knowledge to specific situations" (1987, p. 3). Discussion, he claims, "puts the students in an active learning mode, challenges them to accept substantial responsibility for their own education, and gives them first-hand appreciation of, and experience with, the application of knowledge to practice."

Experts agree that leading a productive discussion is among the most challenging and demanding tasks of an instructor–and one of the most satisfying when things go well. Davis (1993, p. 63) observes:

A good give-and-take discussion can produce unmatched learning experiences as students articulate their ideas, respond to their classmates' points, and develop skills in evaluating the evidence for their own and others' positions. Initiating and sustaining a lively productive discussion are among the most challenging of activities for an instructor.

But too many well-meaning teachers embark on class discussion with the overly simplistic goal of getting students to participate. Participation is a necessary but hardly sufficient condition for learning. Some teachers rationalize their lack of planning by thinking, "Let's just see where the discussion takes us." Occasionally–but only very occasionally–that is a legitimate treasure hunt. More often, students are left tramping through the underbrush of academic density without a clue about what they are searching for or how deeply the treasure might be buried.

Leading a productive discussion takes planning. It is often more work than a lecture because it requires a strategy for dealing with the unexpected as well as the expected. Just as a basketball coach goes into the game with a strategy, one flexible enough to change if conditions demand it but firm enough to reach the goal, so a teacher needs to have his or her eye on the objective. Specifically, what is it that students are expected to learn from the discussion? I have heard teachers emerge from a classroom discussion perfectly happy that it was lively and spirited. Yet basketball players running energetically up and down the court with lots of enthusiasm and broad participation but unmindful of the goal are no more likely to win the game than students are to learn from a discussion that is spirited but off the mark, seemingly headed nowhere. Yes, of course, one wants spirit, activity, and enthusiasm; but the challenge of the learning-centered classroom goes beyond all that.

I vividly remember a lesson about goal-directed discussions that I learned as a participant in a faculty seminar on the discussion method, led by Professor Christensen at Harvard. The seminar was very popular with faculty across all departments, and there was always a waiting list of professors of all levels of experience wanting to learn more about effective teaching by the discussion method. Characteristically, Professor Christensen was the kindly, sensitive master teacher, subtly and skillfully directing the discussion.

So we were considerably surprised one day–and some of us a bit upset–when he ignored a young history professor who had had his hand up for some period of time. Others had been immediately called on. It was certainly not that Professor Christensen did not see the young man, nor was he being disregarded because he talked too much or made irrelevant comments. Why then did the instructor not call on him? After everyone had a chance to become thoroughly puzzled, Professor Christensen addressed our concern. "Yes," he said, "I saw his hand go up early on, and it remained up through four or five other comments. This was the clue to me that his comment pertained to points made four or five comments back and was unlikely to build on the current direction and move it forward."

If the goal of the discussion is to collect a number of different perspectives, then calling on people in turn seems fair and democratic. But at some point, the discussion has to have direction and a goal. The accepted practice of discussion leaders in classrooms is for the leader to call on people in turn. The same is true, at least in most of my experience, with professional committee work. So often a discussion has been robbed of any goal-directed momentum by a discussion leader saying to a sea of waving hands,

"OK, first Dick, then Maria, then Eduardo, then Chauna." Each of these participants then makes his own point, rarely building on the previous point and sometimes not even listening to it. It is like that coach saying to her team, "OK, the first time we get within range, Elnora will shoot, then it will be Cindy's turn, and then Leslie's," with no regard to strategic placement of the players or their ability to work as a team. Since developing teamwork skills is a legitimate educational goal–useful on the job, in civic participation, and as a valuable lifelong learning skill–it is not inappropriate to teach students how to pass the conversational ball.

Three Dimensions of Discussion

A class discussion has three dimensions: content (what the class is about), process (how the class is functioning), and people (who is involved in the process) (Kasulis, 1982). Content is pretty obvious. In fact, most new teachers are overprepared with respect to content. Process distresses many teachers. They recognize when students are not engaged, when one student dominates, when things get argumentative, wandering, or muddled. Much of the problem, say the experts, lies in lack of structure and planning. Millis and Cottell (1998) caution that "when structure is lacking or haphazard, which may have occurred too often in students' previous group work experiences, students wander off task: uncommitted learners revel in the opportunity to 'blow it off,' as more serious students chafe at the wasted time and question the validity of small-group work" (p. 70).

Discussion is more likely to be productive if there is a flexible plan to start with–structured enough to accomplish the goals, but adaptable enough to take advantage of unexpected events. A process plan for a single class may well include successive goals. One example might be to surface a wide variety of perspectives, then to introduce dialectical controversy, then to articulate positions, and finally to reach group consensus.

The third component of discussion is the people involved. Experienced teachers know that no two classes are ever the same. Kasulis (1982, p. 40) contends that "to prepare for a class discussion without taking into consideration the personalities, strengths, and needs of the people in the course is to depersonalize teaching." Some students think quickly, others need more time; some students relate to the anecdotal, others are more analytical; some quote text, others are predictably unconventional. "Much can be gained by calling on the right person at the right time," says Kasulis (1982, p. 41). This is, of course, what Professor Christenson was doing when he resisted the easy temptation to call on people "in turn."

Let us turn now to some practical tips to improve the quality of learning, using the "powerful forces" for learning identified in the research.

"Powerful Forces" for Learning

Classroom discussions would be conducted quite differently than they are today were we to apply the forces for producing learning that have been identified through research, specifically, activity, cooperation, diversity, expectations, interaction, and responsibility.[1] Following a brief discussion of the research and rationale for each of these forces, I will offer some practical tips that have been devised by classroom teachers and reported in various places in the literature. These tips are also available on the Internet via POD@listserv.nd.edu, an exchange of practical advice by those working for the improvement of teaching and learning in higher education.

Activity: Promoting Active Learning

Perhaps the single most important concept to emerge from both neurological and cognitive research in recent years is that people build their own minds by actively constructing the mental network that connects and organizes bits of information. The brain follows the principles of Darwinian competition; it gains strength through the constant activity of making neural connections, and it

---

[1] Although researchers and theoreticians often make precise semantic distinctions between cooperative, collaborative, and interactive learning, I shall use the term "interactive" to include all formats that involve student-to-student communication.

systematically eliminates connections or synapses that are seldom or never used. "Use it or lose it" is demonstrably true, when it comes to developing the capacity of the mind to learn throughout life.

Cognitive scientists reach essentially the same conclusions as the neuroscientists about the necessity for active learning. They build their theory on the concept of the schema as a working mental structure, constantly changing and growing. Each new event, filtered by perception into the schema, is organized and connected to the existing structure to create meaning. One of Piaget's remarkable contributions to our understanding of learning is that children's cognitive structures are not preformed, but rather are constructed as a result of their own mental activity. Children quite literally "build" their own minds. (See Cross Paper # 3, 1999, for further discussion.)

Learners who are actively working their brains to create complex neural connections are building learning capacity. The task of educators is to provide the conditions conducive to growth. People interested in physical fitness today select the gym that provides the best conditions for "working out." They are well aware that the hard work of developing physical fitness must be done by them, but they expect the gym to provide knowledgeable trainers, proper equipment, support and encouragement, and the feeling of belonging to a community of physical fitness buffs that share their interests and commitment.

Ah, would that colleges shared that image! Actually, the national craze for physical fitness is relatively new, and it is only recently that a knowledgeable constituency has grown to demand the services and conditions that promote physical fitness. Fortunately, education is now receiving high recognition from the general public, as well as among politicians and employers. Interest in how to provide the conditions that promote learning is at an all-time peak. There has been a surge in new equipment and new pedagogies, and interest is growing in some of the more active pedagogies such as learning communities and collaborative learning. (See Cross Papers #3 and #4.) But today's high interest in promoting active learning has surfaced a variety of simple low-tech strategies that have been developed over the years by classroom teachers. Some of these, specifically related to promoting active learning, are reported below.

Tips for Promoting Active Learning in Classroom Discussion

- Provocative questions are strategic ways of engaging students in discussion. The following list of question stems includes examples that require thought, critical thinking, and analysis and, therefore, promote active learning:

  - What are the strengths and weaknesses of _____ & _____?
  - What is the difference between _____ & _____?
  - Explain why _____ (or, Explain how _____.)
  - What would happen if _____?
  - What is the next step in _____?
  - What is a new example of _____?
  - What are the implications of _____?
  - What do we already know about _____?
  - Why is _____ important?
  - How does _____ apply in everyday life?
  - What are the arguments against _____?

- Preparing good, discussable questions is a powerful learning experience, as anyone who tries to design questions using the stems above will quickly discover. Why not let students learn by preparing questions that they would like to hear discussed in class? Some teachers take time early in the semester to ask the class to develop criteria for good discussion questions. The criteria are listed and distributed to students for reference whenever they are asked to develop questions for class discussion.

- It is hard to launch a discussion if students haven't read the assignment. Try formulating a few questions as part of the assignment, so that students know they are responsible and have a chance to think about questions ahead of time. This technique is especially helpful in getting participation from some of the more reticent students.

- Provide adequate wait time for students to formulate responses–at least 3-5 seconds, which is roughly the time it takes to chant "Baa baa black sheep, have you any wool." Most teachers wait less than one second before repeating, elaborating, or answering the question themselves. Bonwell and Eison (1991, p. 28) advise that "the single most important action a teacher can take after asking a question is simply to keep quiet." To fill what seems (to teachers) like a long period of silence, you might suggest that students jot down some key notions for their response.

- To advance and deepen a discussion, use questions that build on student comments, for example, "Can you say more about that? Given what you have just said, what do you think the next step might be? Can you give an example of where or how that might apply? How would you respond to Harry's comment?

- Try to avoid reaching agreement too soon. Much of the point of discussion is to expose students to different perspectives and ways of thinking about the question.

Interaction

After reviewing more than 500 research studies pertaining to teaching and learning in college classrooms, psychologists at the University of Michigan concluded that the answer to the question, "What is the most effective method of teaching?" is, "It depends on the goal, the student, the content, and the teacher." But the next best answer is, "students teaching other students" (McKeachie, Pintrich, Lin, & Smith, 1986, p. 63).

College graduates agree. They frequently report that some of their richest learning experiences in college came from interacting with their fellow students. Since the busy schedules of adult students at community colleges do not offer much opportunity to interact with peers outside of class, it is especially important to provide opportunities for peer interaction in class. Researchers report a "very strong relationship" between the number of small classes (15 or fewer people) taken by students and their satisfaction with their overall academic experience (Light, 2001). Thus, community colleges might do well to capitalize on one of their biggest advantages over large state universities. That advantage is that their smaller class size makes student-to-student interaction in the classroom quite feasible–and quite desirable.

Many techniques that call for critical thinking, argumentation, analysis, marshalling of evidence, and the like may be used in a variety of situations from large lectures to individual writing assignments, but they are especially effective when students challenge their peers. Interactive learning can involve as few as two students comparing notes for a few minutes following a lecture or reading assignment, or it may involve longer task assignments to a small interactive group, usually consisting of four to five students. (See Cross Paper #4.)

It is important to keep in mind that learning is the goal in the learning-centered classroom. It is enhanced in a challenging yet supportive environment that keeps students aware that the purpose of their interactions is to help one another do their best learning. A sampling of some techniques for involving students in productive conversations with their peers follows.

Techniques for Promoting Interactive Learning

- **Learning Cells**. Students learn in pairs, alternating between asking and answering questions about a reading assignment.[2] One student begins by asking the first question. After response by the second student, the first student offers corrections and additional information. Students alternate in asking and answering questions. A variation is for students to read different assignments and "teach" their partners the essentials of their readings,

---

[2] The class may agree ahead of time on questions to be discussed by students in their learning cells or by the teacher.

checking for understanding by asking questions (McKeachie, 1994, p. 146-7).

- **Think-Pair-Share**. Think-Pair-Share allows students time to organize information and articulate their thoughts after listening to a lecture or completing a reading assignment. Students think for a few minutes about a question posed by the instructor and then discuss their thoughts with a peer. Together, they create a joint response by building on each other's ideas. Responses may be shared with the whole class (Millis, 1998, pp. 72-78).

- **Believing and Doubting**. Students in small groups are asked to generate reasons for arguments supporting or doubting a controversial statement provided by the instructor (Bean, 1996, p. 157). In a similar technique labeled **Structured Disagreement** (Light, 2001, p. 48), the instructor poses a controversial issue and assigns groups to argue a particular perspective.

- **Case Studies**. Case studies are among the most popular and enduring methods for getting students involved in problem solving and teamwork. Their use has spread well beyond professional fields such as law and business to include the humanities and, especially, writing. (See Bean, 1996.) A well-designed case requires analysis, problem solving, decision-making, and justification. If a case involves different roles, students may be asked to present arguments from their assigned perspective.

Diversity

Diversity has become a major issue in higher education. The courts have been debating whether affirmative action is really an access issue or a quality-of-learning issue. A Michigan court recently rejected the defense of affirmative action as a way to right decades of wrongful discrimination, but defended it on the grounds that diversity of the student body results in a better education for *all* students. In an urgent call for more research on the benefits of diversity, John Friedl (1999, p. 45) says that "the best chance colleges and universities have for overcoming legal challenges to racial preferences in admissions is to demonstrate that their policies confer educational benefits on all students, majority and minority alike."

We in education, however, have made it hard for the courts to defend diversity as a learning opportunity for all. The research evidence for better learning with increased diversity is indicative, but frankly, it is not strong. I suspect that the reason it is not strong is, in part, because we have made such poor use of diversity to promote learning. Rather than regarding diversity as a learning opportunity to be utilized, we regard it as a problem to be solved. We have given too much attention to the mere presence of obvious marks of diversity—skin color, age, gender, disability, etc.—and not enough to diversity of background, perspective, and opinion. A catalog showing students of color mingling and strolling together on campus often has to be staged for the photo shoot. The picture of students of color sitting next to one another in class represents societal progress. But such a scenario has little effect on learning without conscious and deliberate effort to challenge students to interact with one another to produce critical thinking, problem-solving, flexibility, tolerance, values, and all the other things that we talk about as outcomes of a good education.

Remember, however, that the learning advantages of diversity in the classroom derive from more than ethnicity or race. The diversity of the community college population on characteristics of age, experience, socioeconomic background, and level of academic accomplishment make it an especially rich environment for students to learn from one another.

Techniques for Capitalizing on Diversity

- Students often have very different perspectives on the role of education in their lives. Older and younger students expect different things; first-generation students may have very different perspectives from students who have been exposed to higher education via parents or siblings; minority and immigrant students may have different expectations from those of majority students. Try engaging students in conversations about what they want out of college or, more specifically, out of a given class. Students might be asked on the first or second day of class to jot down two or three learning goals for that class, and then to discuss these with peers. (This is a group-based modification of **Goal Ranking and Matching** discussed in Angelo and Cross, 1993, pp. 290-294.)

- Peer tutoring has advantages for both advanced and less advanced learners. Peer tutoring is especially effective when students are in the process of revising first drafts of a writing assignment.

- Research shows that men and women have different ways of learning from small group interactions. Women are more likely to *collect* ideas, whereas men are more likely to *debate* them (Belenky et al., 1986). Ask students to write one good idea that they got from the group discussion and one idea that they would like to debate.

- Ask students to reflect on the *process* of interacting with persons from different ethnic backgrounds. What kinds of issues promoted *unity* of perspective and experience, and which issues surfaced *differences* in perspective? Did the discussion *change* any views previously held?

- Students might be asked to write a dialogue, using different points of view, between characters in a novel or reading assignment. A slight variation is to give a reading assignment presenting a controversial viewpoint and ask students to be prepared to tell why they agree or disagree (Light, 2001, p. 49). Still another variation is to give an assignment on a controversial issue and ask students to be prepared to defend either position. Assign positions randomly for class discussion or a test question.

- As appropriate to the discipline, teachers can do much to develop topics or term papers that explore different cultural contributions and perspectives (Davis, 1993, p. 48). Students might be asked to interview their peers on campus who are from diverse backgrounds, on an issue of campus concern.

Responsibility

While many community college teachers are happy when students assume personal responsibility for doing the assignments and participating in class, the learning-centered classroom requires students to assume *responsibility* for their own learning–in the fullest sense of the word. Just as teachers in the learning college must go beyond presenting instruction, so students in the learning college must go beyond completing assignments. Research suggests that the best learners are aware of themselves as learners. They self-assess their understanding and use effective strategies to manage their own learning process.

Metacognition is the term used to refer to students' awareness and knowledge about their own learning. Good learners are able to watch themselves in the process of learning; they can step back and reflect on how they learn: *What is effective and what is not?* Sometimes called the executive function of the mind, metacognition involves the use of learning strategies such as planning, monitoring understanding, and self-regulation. Evidence shows that such basic learning strategies can be taught (Pintrich, 1988). While teaching such metacognitive skills is often considered the traditional function of study skills courses, teachers of any subject can foster personal responsibility for learning through some fairly simple techniques, some of which are described below.

Techniques for Encouraging Student Acceptance of Responsibility for Learning

- **Reflection**. To help students become aware of themselves as learners, a teacher might stop a lecture or discussion briefly and ask them to reflect on what they were doing at the time and how their behavior helped or hindered their learning. Students might be asked to write down any insights they have gained about their own learning. The teacher may collect the papers as short anonymous notes, thus adding to teacher understanding of learning behaviors (Angelo & Cross, 1993, p. 303).

- **Talking Chips**. This technique is useful in making students aware of their responsibility to the group. Students in a small group discussion are each given a specified number of tokens or chips to surrender when they make a contribution. Students who tend to dominate end up running out of chips, while reticent students are encouraged to participate by using the chips piled in front of them. Talking Chips may be most effective when there is a problem with equitable distribution of responsibility (Millis & Cottell, 1998, pp. 98-99).

- **Directed Paraphrasing**. In this technique, students are directed to paraphrase part of the lesson for a specific audience and purpose, using their own words. In many paraprofessional and service disciplines, the ability to translate academic information to practical uses is an essential skill. For example, students in a course in gerontological nursing might be asked to explain–in one or two sentences, and as they might inform a dying but lucid patient–what they have learned about hospice care's possible advantages over hospital or home care (Angelo & Cross, 1993, pp. 232-235).

Expectations

Expectation is listed as one of the six powerful forces for learning because it is fundamental to student motivation. It is especially important in community colleges, where many students have doubts about their ability to succeed in college. They enter college and the classroom with low expectations for their own success.

Both teacher and student need to plan for success. Research suggests that tasks where the student's chance of success is about

50-50 are the most motivating—easy enough to offer a realistic chance of success, but hard enough to generate a sense of accomplishment when the task is completed successfully. If a task is too easy, a grade too generous, praise too effusive, then students' basic doubts about their own ability may only be exacerbated. The students may infer that the teacher shares these doubts about their ability to perform well in college. If the task is too difficult, anxiety and discouragement are the results.

For students who lack self-confidence, it is important to demonstrate that success springs from the student's own ability and effort. "Success alone is not enough," says University of Michigan psychologist Bill McKeachie. "For students who lack a sense of efficacy, teachers must not only provide situations where success occurs but also give students opportunities to undertake challenging tasks on their own, to prove to themselves that they can achieve" (1994, p. 352). McKeachie sums up the teacher's role in raising expectations and accomplishment with these words: "When students are confident that they have the answers and can achieve their goals without effort, you need to provide challenges; for students who lack confidence you need to provide support and opportunities to show progress and achieve success." (1994, p. 353.) (See Cross Paper #5 for further discussion of the role of expectations in motivation.)

Techniques for Raising Expectations and Enhancing Motivation

- **Quiz Bowl**. Researchers agree that moderate competition may be helpful in increasing motivation and engagement, while individual competition often provokes anxiety, resentment and discouragement—especially among those with low self-confidence. To capitalize on the positive aspects of competition, divide the class into teams, with team members consulting on the answers to previously prepared questions. The quiz bowl format is especially productive when used in a test review (McKeachie, 1994, p. 356).

- **Choice**. Offer flexibility and choice when possible. Choice (e.g., in papers and discussion topics) gives students a sense of control, and lets them choose topics or tasks where they face a challenge with reasonable expectations of success.

- **Pacing**. Pace learning so that each step offers some newness and only a moderate risk of failure (McKeachie, 1994, p. 353).

- **Goal-Setting**. Have students write out their goals for your course. Encourage them to monitor their own progress, and provide prompt and accurate feedback.

Conclusions

There are numerous routes to designing a learning-centered classroom. Teachers need to find a fit between methods appropriate to their discipline, their own competence and comfort level, and the successful promotion of student learning. For some teachers and in some disciplines, this means radical innovation, experimentation, and assessment to determine how much and how well students are learning the goals established for the course. For others it may mean experimentation, improvement, and assessment within fairly traditional pedagogies. For all community college teachers, it means that the ultimate criterion of success is student learning.

We do know the important correlates of learning. We do know what a learning-centered classroom should look like. Students have the best opportunities for successful learning when they take **responsibility** for engaging **actively** in **interaction** with the teacher and a **diversity** of fellow students, with the **expectation** of succeeding in tasks that are challenging and represent a sense of accomplishment.

REFERENCES

Angelo, T. A., & Cross, K. P. (1993). *Classroom Assessment Techniques: A Handbook for College Teachers*, Second Edition. San Francisco: Jossey-Bass.

Barr, R. B., & Tagg, J. (1995). From Teaching to Learning: A New Paradigm for Undergraduate Education. *Change*, November/December, 13-25.

Bean, J. C. (1996). *Engaging Ideas: The Professor's Guide to Integrating Writing, Critical Thinking, and Active Learning in the Classroom*. San Francisco: Jossey-Bass.

Belenky, M. F., Clinchy, B. M., Goldberger, N. R., & Tarule, J. M. (1986). *Women's Ways of Knowing: The Development of Self, Voice, and Mind*. New York: Basic Books.

Bonwell, C. C., & Eison, J. A. (1991). *Active Learning*. Washington, DC: ERIC Clearinghouse on Higher Education, George Washington University.

Chickering, A. W., & Gamson, Z. F. (1987). Seven Principles for Good Practice in Undergraduate Education. *The Wingspread Journal*, 9(2). See also *AAHE Bulletin*, March, 1987.

Christensen, C. R. (1987). *Teaching and the Case Method*. Boston: Harvard Business School.

Cross, K. P. (2000). *Collaborative Learning 101: Cross Paper #4*. Mission Viejo, CA: League for Innovation in the Community College.

Cross, K. P. (1999). *Learning is About Making Connections: Cross Paper #3*. Mission Viejo, CA: League for Innovation in the Community College.

Cross, K. P. (1998). *Opening Windows on Learning: Cross Paper Number 2*. Mission Viejo, CA: League for Innovation in the Community College.

Davis, B. G. (1993). *Tools for Teaching*. San Francisco: Jossey-Bass.

Friedl, J. (July/August 1999). Needed: Documentation of How Affirmative Action Benefits All Students. *Change*, 31(4), 40-45.

Kasulis, T. P. (1982). Questioning. In M. M. Gullette (Ed.), *The Art and Craft of Teaching*. Cambridge, MA: Harvard-Danforth Center for Teaching and Learning.

Light, R. J. (2001). *Making the Most of College: Students Speak Their Minds*. Cambridge, MA: Harvard University Press.

McKeachie, W. J. (1994). *Teaching Tips*, Ninth Edition. Lexington, MA: D.C. Heath.

Millis, B. J., & Cottell, P. G. (1998). *Cooperative Learning for Higher Education Faculty*. Phoenix: Oryx Press.

National Commission on Excellence in Education (1983). *A Nation at Risk*. Washington, DC: U. S. Department of Education.

O'Banion, T. (1999). The Learning College: Both Learner and Learning Centered. *Learning Abstracts*, 2(2).

Pintrich, P. R. (1988). Student Learning and College Teaching. In R. E. Young & K. E. Eble (Eds.), *New Directions for Teaching and Learning*, No. 33. San Francisco: Jossey-Bass.

K. Patricia Cross

K. Patricia Cross is Professor of Higher Education, Emerita at the University of California, Berkeley, and Senior League Fellow at the League for Innovation in the Community College. Cross has had a varied and distinguished career as a university administrator (Assistant Dean of Women at the University of Illinois and Dean of Students at Cornell University), researcher (Distinguished Research Scientist at Educational Testing Service and Research Educator at The Center for Research and Development in Higher Education, University of California, Berkeley), and teacher (Professor and Chair of the Department of Administration, Planning, and Social Policy at the Harvard Graduate School of Education and Professor of Higher Education, University of California, Berkeley).

The author of nine books and more than 200 articles and chapters, Cross has been recognized for her scholarship by election to the National Academy of Education, receipt of the E. F. Lindquist Award from the American Educational Research Association, the Sidney Suslow Award from the Association for Institutional Research, and the Howard Bowen Distinguished Career Award from the Association for the Study of Higher Education.

Past Chair of the Board of the American Association for Higher Education, she has received a number of awards for leadership in education, among them the 1990 Leadership Award from the American Association of Community and Junior Colleges and the 1990 award for outstanding contributions to the improvement of instruction from the National Council of Instructional Administrators. She has been awarded 14 honorary doctorates and is listed in *Who's Who in America*.

Cross serves on the editorial boards of six national and international journals of higher education. She has lectured on American higher education widely in the United States and abroad in England, France, Sweden, Germany, the former Soviet Union, Japan, Australia, Hong Kong, and Holland. Her primary areas of interest are adult learning, changing college student populations, and the improvement of teaching and learning in higher education.

Cross received her bachelor's degree in mathematics from Illinois State University and her master's degree and doctorate in social psychology from the University of Illinois.

K. Patricia Cross
Professor of Higher Education, Emerita
University of California, Berkeley
Phone and Fax: 510-527-9020
patcross@socrates.berkeley.edu
Mailing address:
904 Oxford Street, Berkeley, CA 94707